43537488

Struck by LIGHTNING!

Disaster SURVIVORS

by Stephen Person

Consultant: John Jensenius
National Weather Service, NOAA

BEARPORT
PUBLISHING

New York, New York

Credits

Cover, © Chris Price/iStockphoto; 4, © Greg Von Doersten/Aurora/Getty Images; 5, © SuperStock; 6, © Leo Larson; 7, © Leo Larson; 8, © Ethan Hill; 9, Courtesy of the European Space Agency, Image by Christophe Carreau; 10, © Nelson Medina/Photo Researchers, Inc.; 12, © AP Images/Ed Andrieski; 13L, Courtesy of Ruth Lyon-Bateman/NOAA; 13R, Courtesy of Linda Cooper; 14, © Warren Faidley/Weatherstock; 15, © The Granger Collection, New York; 16, © Ray Manley/SuperStock; 18, © Reuters/Landov; 19, © Scott T. Smith Dembinsky Photo Associates; 20, Courtesy of Cgoodwin; 21, © Paul Katz/Index Stock Imagery/Photolibrary; 22, © Richard Gwin/Lawrence Journal-World; 23, © Dennis Hallinan/Alamy; 24, Courtesy of Shenandoah National Park; 25, © David Woodfall/Still Pictures/Peter Arnold Inc.; 26, © Ilene MacDonald/Alamy; 27, Courtesy of National Weather Service/Lightning Safety/NOAA; 28T, © AP Images/Dale Sparks; 28B, Courtesy of Edward J. Rupke/Lightning Technologies, Inc.; 29, © Built Images/SuperStock.

Publisher: Kenn Goin
Editorial Director: Adam Siegel
Creative Director: Spencer Brinker
Design: Dawn Beard Creative
Photo Researcher: Daniella Nilva

Library of Congress Cataloging-in-Publication Data

Person, Stephen.
  Struck by lightning! / by Stephen Person.
    p. cm. — (Disaster survivors)
  Includes bibliographical references and index.
  ISBN-13: 978-1-936087-47-1 (lib. bdg.)
  ISBN-10: 1-936087-47-2 (lib. bdg.)
 1. Lightning—Juvenile literature. 2. Lightning conductors—Juvenile literature. 3. Lightning protection—Juvenile literature. I. Title.
 QC966.5.P47 2010
 551.56'32—dc22

                                        2009031207

For more information, write to Bearport Publishing Company, Inc., 101 Fifth Avenue, Suite 6R, New York, New York 10003. Printed in the United States of America in North Mankato, Minnesota.

112009
090309CGB

10 9 8 7 6 5 4 3 2 1

Contents

A Mountaintop Strike

It was late afternoon on July 26, 2003. Rod Liberal and his friends were nearing the top of Grand Teton Mountain in Wyoming. This was Rod's first time climbing the mountain, and he was excited to reach its **summit**.

Climbers near the 13,770-foot (4,197-m) peak of Grand Teton Mountain.

As Rod clung to the side of a cliff, he saw dark clouds rolling toward him. Suddenly, he heard a buzzing sound. He felt the hair on his arms stand up. Then there was a burst of light as a bolt of lightning struck his chest and blew him off the mountain. Luckily, he was attached to the cliff by a rope. He swung in the air, thousands of feet above the ground.

Lightning strikes in Grand Teton National Park, Wyoming

About 100 bolts of lightning strike Earth's surface every second.

Rescue in the Sky

The lightning strike **paralyzed** Rod's left arm and right leg. He was in terrible pain, and thought his back might be broken. He tried to scream, but could not make a sound. "Hold on, buddy!" one of Rod's friends called down from the mountain above. "Just keep breathing." Rod's friends used a cell phone to call **park rangers** for help.

Park rangers prepare to rescue Rod on the side of the mountain.

As the sun began to set, Rod heard a helicopter. Park rangers had come to rescue him. They secured Rod to a basket attached to the helicopter and flew him to a hospital. "We didn't think he would survive the night," one of the rangers said. "He was really hurt. He took the full blast of the lightning."

A helicopter picked Rod up and flew him to a hospital.

Lightning is one of the leading causes of weather-related deaths in the United States. Most years, it kills more people than hurricanes or snowstorms.

7

Lucky to Be Alive

Doctors found severe burns on Rod's chest, as well as damage to his lungs. Rod spent about two months recovering in the hospital. It took him another four months to relearn how to sit up and walk.

Rod and his family relax at their home in Utah. Rod still plays hockey with his friends, though his legs are not as strong as they used to be.

Around 60 people are killed by lightning each year in the United States.

It may seem amazing that anyone could be hit by lightning and live. However, most people do survive lightning strikes. According to Dr. Mary Ann Cooper, a leading expert on lightning strike **injuries**, "Ninety percent of lightning victims survive, but often with **disability**."

Lightning doesn't occur just on Earth. It also strikes other planets such as Jupiter, Saturn, and Venus. This picture was created by an artist to show what lightning on Venus might look like.

A Blinding Bolt

Lightning can strike a person doing much more ordinary things than mountain climbing. In 1983, Linda Cooper parked outside the post office in Fort Lauderdale, Florida. It was a gray, rainy day. As Linda stepped out of her car, a bolt of lightning smacked her head and knocked her down to the wet sidewalk.

A lightning storm in Florida

There are more lightning strikes per square mile (sq km) in Florida than in any other state.

"All I remember is a blinding white light," Linda said, "and the loudest sound I have ever heard or could ever imagine hearing." Badly confused, she stood up and walked into the post office. After mailing her package, she got back into her car and drove to an exercise class!

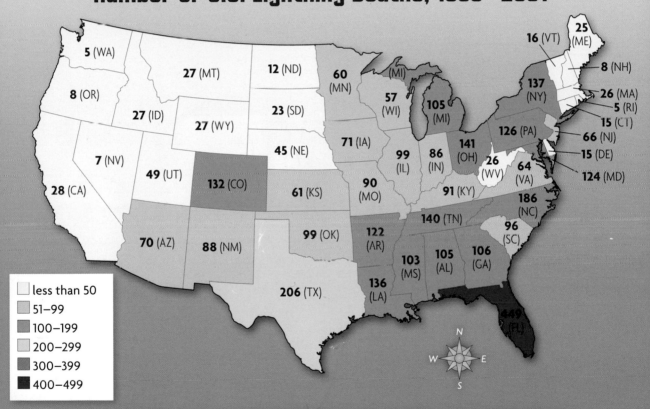

Number of U.S. Lightning Deaths, 1959–2007

5 (WA)
27 (MT)
12 (ND)
60 (MN)
(MI)
16 (VT)
25 (ME)
8 (OR)
57 (WI)
137 (NY)
8 (NH)
27 (ID)
23 (SD)
105 (MI)
26 (MA)
27 (WY)
126 (PA)
5 (RI)
71 (IA)
15 (CT)
45 (NE)
99 (IL)
86 (IN)
141 (OH)
66 (NJ)
7 (NV)
49 (UT)
132 (CO)
26 (WV)
64 (VA)
15 (DE)
28 (CA)
61 (KS)
90 (MO)
91 (KY)
124 (MD)
186 (NC)
140 (TN)
96 (SC)
70 (AZ)
88 (NM)
99 (OK)
122 (AR)
103 (MS)
105 (AL)
106 (GA)
206 (TX)
136 (LA)
449 (FL)

Legend:
- less than 50
- 51–99
- 100–199
- 200–299
- 300–399
- 400–499

N
W   E
S

In the United States, Florida has had the most deaths caused by lightning.

After the Strike

Just like Linda, many lightning strike victims feel fine right after being hit. In the days that follow, however, victims often begin to feel sick. Several days after being struck, Linda started having pounding headaches.

This Colorado teenager and his mother show his shoe and shirt, both burned by lightning while he was wearing them. Luckily, he suffered only minor injuries.

Because of air and ice movements within the cloud, the lower part of the cloud becomes negatively charged. The ground below has negative and positive charges. The negative charges in the cloud are attracted to positive charges on the ground. When the difference between the negative charges in the cloud and the positive charges on the ground becomes too great, a giant spark of electricity may shoot out of the cloud and strike the ground. This spark is called lightning.

How Lightning Forms

Negative electrical charges build up at the bottom of storm clouds.

Electrical charges burst from the cloud in the form of lightning bolts.

Bolts of lightning are usually about 1 to 2 inches (2.5 to 5 cm) wide. They can be more than 20 miles (32 km) long.

✚ positive electrical charges
━ negative electrical charges

Listening For Thunder

When people see lightning they also often hear thunder. Why? The sound of thunder is created by lightning. A bolt of lightning heats the air around it, forcing the air to **expand** very quickly. The fast-moving air creates the booming sound of thunder.

Lightning strikes occur throughout the world. A powerful bolt struck this house in South Africa and set it on fire.

Thunder and lightning occur at the exact same moment. People usually see lightning before they hear thunder, however, because light moves much faster than sound. Light travels about 186,000 miles (299,338 km) per second. Sound travels about one mile (1.6 km) in five seconds. As a result, people who are one mile from a lightning bolt will see the flash instantly. They will hear thunder about five seconds later.

Only about 30 percent of all lightning bolts hit the ground. The rest remain in the clouds.

To figure out how many miles away a **thunderstorm** is, count the seconds between the flash of lightning and the sound of thunder. Then divide that number by five. For example, if ten seconds pass between the lightning and thunder, the storm is about two miles (3.2 km) away.

Getting to Safety

Any time people see lightning or hear thunder, they should find **shelter** right away. This means staying away from trees, because lightning often strikes tall objects. Open fields are dangerous, too. In a field, the tallest thing around may be a person. People should also avoid being in water during a storm. Lightning can zip through water and kill anyone touching it.

Lightning often strikes trees and other tall objects as it shoots toward the ground.

Skyscrapers are frequently hit by lightning. The buildings are safe places, however, if they are built with **lightning rods**. A lightning rod is a metal pole that is placed on top of a building, with a wire leading into the earth. When lightning strikes the pole, the electric shock travels down the wire harmlessly into the ground. Benjamin Franklin invented the lightning rod in 1753.

New York City's Empire State Building is struck by lightning about 100 times every year. A lightning rod protects the building and people inside.

Even if a building doesn't have a lightning rod, it can still be a safe place to stay during a thunderstorm if it has wiring and plumbing. The electrical current from lightning will usually travel through a house's wiring or plumbing into the ground.

A Bolt From the Blue

Even if the sky is blue, people should seek safety if thunderstorms are nearby. The sky was blue above the North Carolina bank where Steve Marshburn was working. He was sitting inside a drive-up window when a bolt of lightning shot through the open window and struck his back. "It felt as if someone had hit me with a baseball bat," he said.

In 1989, Steve Marshburn founded Lightning Strike and Electric Shock Survivors. The group helps victims stay in touch and support one another.

This woman holds up the pair of jeans she was wearing when she was struck by lightning.

This kind of lightning strike is what **meteorologists** call a "bolt from the blue." How did it get this name? Some lightning bolts shoot out the side of a cloud. As a result, they can strike the ground up to 25 miles (40 km) away, where skies are blue.

There are 1.2 billion lightning flashes on Earth each year. Some of these occur on sunny days.

The Human Lightning Rod

A person's chances of being hit by lightning in his or her lifetime are 1 in 5,000. Yet that hasn't helped Roy Sullivan. This Virginia park ranger was nicknamed the "human lightning rod" after being struck a world-record seven times!

Roy Sullivan shows a hat that was struck by lightning—while it was on his head!

In 1972, lightning struck Sullivan in the head and set his hair on fire. The quick-thinking ranger poured a bucket of water over his head, putting out the flames.

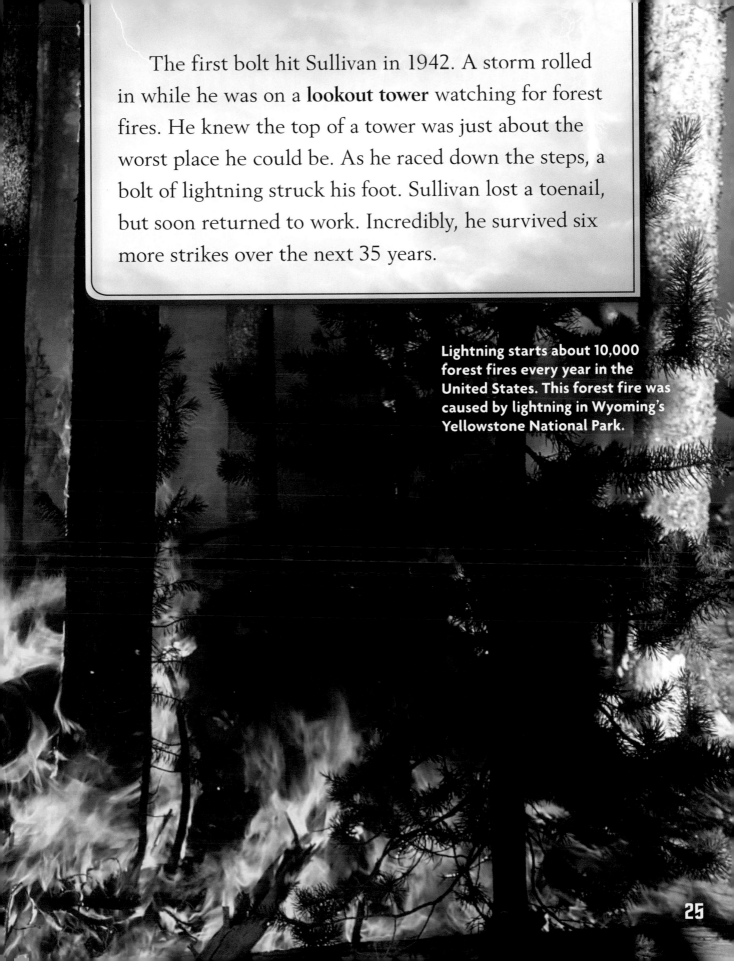

The first bolt hit Sullivan in 1942. A storm rolled in while he was on a **lookout tower** watching for forest fires. He knew the top of a tower was just about the worst place he could be. As he raced down the steps, a bolt of lightning struck his foot. Sullivan lost a toenail, but soon returned to work. Incredibly, he survived six more strikes over the next 35 years.

Lightning starts about 10,000 forest fires every year in the United States. This forest fire was caused by lightning in Wyoming's Yellowstone National Park.

Learning From Lightning

Will anyone ever break Roy Sullivan's record of seven lightning strikes? Carl Mize of Oklahoma is getting close. He has been struck six times. "Some people say I'm unlucky," Carl said. "I think I'm kind of lucky to be alive."

Fortunately for Carl and other people, the number of injuries and deaths from lightning strikes has been falling in recent years. One reason is that people know more about lightning safety. Better **weather forecasts** also help people avoid getting caught in thunderstorms.

Meteorologists use computers to track thunderstorms so that they can warn people if they are in danger.

Rod Liberal knows the danger of lightning as well as anyone. More than six years after his mountaintop rescue in 2003, Rod is slowly but surely recovering from his strike. He even climbed Grand Teton Mountain again. "Reaching the summit," Rod said, "was the best feeling in the world."

People know more about lightning safety today than ever before.

A woman who had been climbing with Rod was killed when a lightning strike caused her heart to stop beating. This is the most common cause of death in lightning strikes.

Famous Strikes

Lightning bolts usually strike just one person at a time. Throughout history, however, a few lightning bolts have caused major disasters.

Rhodes, Greece, 1856

- Lightning struck a church tower. The electricity traveled down the tower and into the basement, where barrels of gunpowder were stored.
- The gunpowder exploded, destroying nearby buildings and killing about 4,000 people.
- Scientists and historians think this was the deadliest lightning strike in history.

West Virginia, 2006

- A lightning bolt hit the ground near a coal mine, causing gas in the mine to explode.
- Part of the mine collapsed, trapping 13 miners underground. Only one of the miners survived.
- This tragedy has become known as the Sago Mine Disaster.

Randal McCloy was the only survivor of the Sago Mine Disaster.

Maryland, 1963

- A lightning bolt hit a jet airplane in the skies over Maryland. The bolt lit fuel in the tank, sparking an explosion.
- The left wing of the plane was blown off, causing the plane to crash. All 81 people on board were killed.
- Most large airplanes are struck by lightning at least once every year. Today's planes have safety features that are designed to prevent sparks from reaching fuel tanks or damaging a plane's computers.

Scientists test the effects of lightning on new airplanes.

Lightning Safety

Here are some lightning safety tips from the National Weather Service:

☑ Always check weather reports before planning outdoor activities. While outside, watch for thunderstorms.

☑ Remember to follow the advice of the National Weather Service: "When thunder roars, go indoors." Wait at least 30 minutes after hearing the last rumble of thunder before leaving shelter.

☑ The safest locations during a thunderstorm are houses or other solid buildings. Tents do not protect people from lightning.

☑ Most people are not struck directly by lightning. Instead, they are usually struck by lightning as it moves along the ground or along metal surfaces or wires. Consequently, don't use corded phones and avoid touching metal pipes or window frames during a storm. Also, do not touch anything that is plugged into the wall.

☑ If someone is struck by lightning, call 911. Don't worry about touching the victim—he or she cannot **electrocute** you.

Open picnic pavilions like this one are not safe places during thunderstorms.

Glossary

disability (*diss*-uh-BIL-i-tee) a condition that makes it hard for a person to do everyday things

electrical charges (i-LEK-truh-kuhl CHARJ-iz) positive or negative charges that can build up on an object; when objects with opposite charges make contact with each other, there is a flow of electricity, sometimes in the form of a spark

electricity (i-lek-TRISS-uh-tee) a form of energy; the flow of electrical power

electrocute (i-LEK-truh-kyoot) to kill with electricity

energy (EN-ur-jee) power that makes machines work and produces heat

expand (ek-SPAND) to increase in size or volume

experiment (ek-SPER-uh-ment) a scientific test that is set up to find the answer to a question

injuries (IN-juh-reez) harm done to a person's body

lightning rods (LITE-ning RODZ) tools used to protect buildings from damage by lightning strikes

lookout tower (LUK-*out* TOW-ur) an elevated platform from which park rangers can watch for forest fires

meteorologists (*mee*-tee-ur-OL-oh-jists) scientists who study weather and weather prediction

paralyzed (PA-ruh-lized) caused something to be unable to move or act

park rangers (PARK RAYN-jurz) workers in charge of protecting parks and coming to the aid of park visitors

shelter (SHEL-tur) a place that provides safety from danger

summit (SUHM-it) the top of a mountain

symptoms (SIMP-tuhmz) signs of a disease or other physical problem felt by a person; often feelings of pain or discomfort

theory (THIHR-ee) an idea or belief based on limited information

thunderstorm (THUHN-dur-*storm*) a storm with thunder and lightning

weather forecasts (WETH-ur FOR-kasts) reports about what the weather will be like in the coming hours and days

Bibliography

Daley, Jason. "Struck." *Outside Magazine* (October 2005). http://outside.away.com/outside/features/200510/ rod-liberal-struck-by-lightning-1.html

Friedman, John S. *Out of the Blue: A History of Lightning: Science, Superstition, and Amazing Stories of Survival.* New York: Delacorte Press (2008).

National Geographic/Lightning http://environment.nationalgeographic.com/environment/ natural-disasters/lightning-profile.html

NOAA/National Severe Storms Laboratory http://www.nssl.noaa.gov/primer/lightning/ltg_faq.shtml

Read More

Galiano, Dean. *Thunderstorms and Lightning.* New York: Rosen (2000).

Hamilton, John. *Lightning (Nature's Fury).* Edina, MN: Abdo (2006).

Williams, Brian. *Lightning (What on Earth?).* New York: Children's Press (2005).

Learn More Online

To learn more about lightning, visit
www.bearportpublishing.com/DisasterSurvivors

Index

About the Author

*Stephen Person has written many children's books
about the environment, nature, and history.
He lives with his family in Brooklyn, New York.*